SAP Production Planning Questions, Answers, and Explanations

SAPCOOKBOOK.COM

Please visit our website at www.sapcookbook.com
© 2006 Equity Press all rights reserved.

ISBN 1-933804-09-2

Trademark notices

TABLE OF CONTENTS

SAP PP
Questions, Answers, and Explanations

SAPCOOKBOOK
Equity Press

☞ **QUESTION 1**

Authorization for Costs in Production Order

I have a situation wherein an object allows certain functions that should not be.

For example: I have a role that allows seeing prices and other items that should instead be a 'limited access' function. I don't know how to configure it so that access can be controlled. I assume it should be in the authorizations of the role (TCode= PFCG). However, I don't find any appropriate object for the configuration.

How can I limit the access to costs in the production order?

✍ **ANSWER**

If you are using version 40b, you can limit access to costs (analysis etc), via the production order by not giving access to Report Writer: Report Group (G_803J_GJB).

One other solution could be: Assigning Object K_KEKO responsible for the checking of the authorization for costs.

How can I assign production order without material to standard production order in rework scenario?

☞ QUESTION 2

Assignment of production order

✍ ANSWER

If you are trying to assign the rework order as the initial order so that all the rework order cost would be captured to the initial order, then I suggest the following:

Assign your rework order to the initial order by entering the initial order to the rework order at the "settlement rule" (header). The category should be ORD (order). This should be followed by the order number and the percentage of the cost absorbed by the initial order.

☞ QUESTION 3

Split planned order during MRP run by production version

We have 2 production lines within one plant to produce the same finished product. For planning, we put the planning quantity for finish product in Demand

Management with a daily planning period and differentiated the production line

with a production version. The problem occurs when we run MRP. The system automatically accumulates the requirement in a same day demand. Hence, we need to automatically split the planned order with a different production line.

Since the lot size range is the same, is there a more efficient way as to how we can split the planned order?

✍ ANSWER

If you want to split the planned order by percentage, you can use quota arrangement (meq1).

If you want to split order by capacity, then you might want to use fixed lot size, and finite capacity with option "changing production version on error".

☞ QUESTION 4

Subcontracting

This is the scenario I am faced with:

1. We have a cloth material master number. A stock item and a shirt material master number B also logged as a stock item.
2. We have Created a subcontracting Info Record for the shirt.
3. We have created a Source list for the shirt.
4. We created a bill.

During routing, we have assigned a control key PP02 to operation>elected, the subcontracting check box, and attempted to enter the purchasing info record.

Here, we get the following message:

'Enter info record without material
Message no. CP 561

Diagnosis
You entered a purchasing info record with a material master. This is not acceptable for external processing operation since you are purchasing a service or activity and not a material.

Procedure
Enter a purchasing info record without a material master that has an info record category 0 (normal) or 3 (subcontracting) subcontractor purchasing info records (type "3").'

Note:
If, when you are searching for a suitable info record, you select the search help "info records for external processing", the system automatically displays only the info records without material masters that have the info record category 0 or 3.'

What are we doing incorrectly? What must be done to correct this issue?

Additional info:
The item (say shirt) is a stock item. I want to create a PO on the vendor to manufacture the shirts and issue it with our special material (say cloth) from our stock to make the shirts and receive the shirts into stock. From hereon, no production order will be created.

Am I correct to assume that in this scenario we do not have to couple the info record to the routing, as we would do for an "outside process" for a production order?

✍ Answer

The Info records with material are used if you create purchase orders with the bill of material for subcontracting.
You probably configured it as a production process. Hence, you must not have an info record together with material. You need to create a subcontracting info record without entering a material number. This info record will then need to be entered at your operation.

This is the standard subcontracting process in MM and therefore, no routing is required.

☞ **QUESTION 5**

Using MIGO for Goods Issue Reversals

We are upgrading to 4.6C from 4.0. In 4.0, you can reverse a goods issue to process order using the standard IM transaction MB1A. If you reverse with reference to an order, the system proposes the materials, quantities and batches previously issued against the order. You can then just change the quantity and reverse, for example, only a portion of what was originally issued.

We tried to do this with MIGO (or MIGO_GI), and it doesn't seem to work. MIGO gives you the option to enter the movement type (262, in this case) in the header row, but it doesn't seem to recognize that movement type. When we try to do a 262, the system either proposes the balance of the components which have not been fully issued, or says "document contains no selectable items" if all components have been fully issued. It appears that the system still thinks we are doing a 261, despite the fact that we entered 262 in the movement type field.

We want the system to propose the details of the items that have already been issued (so that it is easier to just change the appropriate quantities), so using the "New items" button and re-entering the material, batch, etc. is not a preferred option. Is there a proper way to do this with MIGO?

✍ **ANSWER**

Try to use Transaction MBST instead. It would factor in the necessary requirements and changes for what you need.

☞ QUESTION **6**

Entries get posted though production order has been closed

Why is it that entries get posted after every month's end under my production order although the order has been closed? The current status is REL CNF DLV PRC BCRQ GMPS MACM SETC VCAL.

I checked again my production order via CO03 and the status is currently set to 1 OPEN for all Act. Is this the reason why? Should I change it to 3 CLSD Closed for all Act?

When you display production order via CO03 you see the order number in the first line followed by the material and then the status. I clicked the "i" icon beside the status and it is there that I see the status OPEN and CLOSED on the right side of the screen.

I also don't see any TECO status in my production order. Where can I find all the status available for production order? Is it in SPRO? What is the path?

✍ ANSWER

It appears from the status that the order is fully confirmed and delivered.

Generally, if Order is having TECO it will not allow any further posting of Cost to the order.

Even in techno status, we can post the entries. If you want to avoid the postings, then close the order.

As a standard, you can still post goods issues and book costs, etc. to a production order while it is at a status TECO. To prevent this, you will have to close the production order, which generally cannot be done until the balance is zero (i.e. settlement has been performed).

Before closing the order you should perform these actions:

Technically complete the order by functions>restrict processing>technically complete on order header screen which will bring techno status of year order, this is required for cost settlement.

Then, create distribution rule for settlement header>settlement rule, Then, settle the order using ko88.tocde which will bring SETC status to year order>then close the order.

After the above corrections, no further postings can be avoided.

SETC is Settlement Rule Created. This status is usually activated when the order is created and an appropriate settlement rule is assigned.

Running settlement does not create a status. You can see the balance of an order (CO02) through menu path – Go to –> Costs –> Balance.

Settlement can be run more than once for an order, so if you do not want any further postings, you have to close the order immediately after settlement. Please note that closing the order will initiate a check to ensure there are no outstanding commitments against the order (invoices, PO's etc). If there are, you will not be able to close the order until these are cleared.

☞ QUESTION 7

Split Production orders

I am using the Split Production order functionality. I created an order # 123. I split this order to create a child order # 321.

Is it possible to further split order # 321 using split order functionality?

✍ ANSWER

Yes, it should be possible to further split the orders. Try it and see.

☞ **QUESTION 8**

'Reverse MRP' for obsolete requirements

One of our customers regularly changes his mid range production plan, deleting the previously created planned orders. The problem is, there might be some purchase orders left in the system, which had already been created based on the MRP run, especially for raw materials with long lead times.

What we're looking for is a report that gives us a list of purchasing documents (requisitions or orders) that have become obsolete and - in the case of purchase orders - should be cancelled, if possible.

Is there something like that (a report that will give us the list) in standard SAP?

Can you use exception messages in MRP?

✍ **ANSWER**

From the MM process point of view, there is not such a thing as an 'obsolete' purchasing documents. There are various standard transactions which can list out the purchase requisitions (ME5A Transaction) or Request for Quotation (Transaction ME4L, ME4M, ME4N) or Purchase Order (Transaction ME2L, ME2M, ME2N). However, whether a certain purchasing document is regarded as 'obsolete' is subject completely to your own justification. Of course, it is feasible to include the status of your purchasing documents (pending versus complete). However, this would require an ABAP development (PO, for instance).

If there is no requirement for the raw material but there is PO still outstanding, it should give you exception message 20 - cancel process. That should be the job of the raw material planner.

☞ QUESTION 9

MRP Run for Material Range

Is it possible to run MRP for a material range? (Not by MRP Controller, PDT Group, etc.)

✍ ANSWER

No, this is not possible. However, SAP provides many solutions for you to manage your MRP run.

Your options for this are to either set up product groups and assign your materials to the relevant product group, or create an MRP group and assign your materials to the relevant MRP group.

You can actually be able to run MRP for a material item (via Transaction MD03 or MD02), for the entire plant (MD01) or for a storage location (via the usage of MRP Area) or for a certain MRP Controller, Material Group or Material Type etc. via the User Exit.

Check the user exit for MRP M61X0001. It can select based on the defined parameter in total planning run (MD01). Sample codes are also available in program LXM61F01.

☞ QUESTION 10

Maintain Alternative Item Group Error

Here is the scenario:

User maintains the substitute material in BOM, A101 is the primary material; B102 is the substitute material, the step as follows:

Tx: CO02 in the A101 item, Alternative Item Group is 01, Priority is 2, Strategy is 2, Usage problem is 0.

In the B102 item, Alternative Item Group is 01, Priority is 2, Strategy is 2, Usage problem is 0.

Hence, the production orders have not committed quantity. What can I do to resolve this?

✍ ANSWER

Basically you should maintain one of your alternate items to be primary with priority 1. You want to check whether the stock is available - if yes, you may want to switch to priority 2.

Then you should maintain your primary to have priority 1, usage problem 100%, and your secondary alternates with priority 2, usage problem 0.

Then you use strategy 1 (100% check) meaning that if availability of primary is not fulfilled, it switches to secondary.

☞ QUESTION **11**

Location of time of transaction MD05

Is there a table in which the TIME of transaction MD05 is saved? And the USER who executed the MRP runs?

✍ ANSWER

I would try using ST03N and look at transaction analysis.

Table MDKP is kept the MRP List header and have the MRP date as one of the fields. Table MDTB is the table for MRP List items.

☞ **QUESTION 12**

Combining two Configurable Materials

One of our customers would like us to ship two different Configurable Materials (different SuperBOMs, different configuration profiles, different classes) to act as a single configurable "system".

My inelegant method was to create a new Configurable Material, SuperBOM, Class; Configuration Profile where I manually entered every bit of data from the two combined materials. While technically this worked, there has to be a better way - one that does not require maintaining several massive (our products are quite involved) SuperBOMs which contain very similar data.

Does anybody have any idea how to proceed and comply with the requirements?

✍ **ANSWER**

No need to go that deep - you can create one superior material that has BOM with the two existing KMATs. The superior material should have each of the classes of the two KMATs assigned to it (SAP will merge them internally).

Your tasks, then, would be:

1) To make sure that where the same characteristic is used in both lower KMATs, they have the same set of possible values;

2) To copy profile-level dependencies into the configuration

profile of the superior material;

3) To create BOM selection conditions for the superior material as needed;

4) If you want to pick the two assemblies separately, set everything up with a sales BOM explosion;

☞ QUESTION 13

BOM Error

Our user has created a BOM for material X.

When he is creating Process Order, he is getting following message:

'No Valid Task List Maintained for Material X Plant P for Selected Criteria'.

Where is the mistake?

✍ ANSWER

The material is to be processed using a task list - & there's no task list / routing / recipe etc available.

Check the following things:

(A) Validity dates maintained in the BOM,routing and production version;
(B) Lot size ranges maintained in the production version;
(C) Order type dependent parameters of that plant;
(D) Check the material assigned to the routing;

☞ **QUESTION 14**

Work center formula

Why do we need different formula for setup requirements and processing time requirements in capacity tap & scheduling tab?

✐ **ANSWER**

These formulas are used for capacity planning and scheduling of orders during execution as well planning of orders and materials.

One formula is used for time calculation of one piece and the other is used for scheduling that is to indicate the number of pieces.

In a nutshell, capacity is used for determining the actual capacity requirements, whereas scheduling is used to determine the basic dates.

☞ QUESTION 15

Variant configuration and BOM

I have three questions:

Can you give me the steps in variant configuration?

How do I create a variant BOM?

✍ ANSWER

[quote="supersubra"]

1. Create first BOM thru transaction code cs01
2. Create second BOM thru same transaction code. You will get a message alternative2 added.

For creating a variant bom, select a "create a variant of" and give the reference of BOM for which you want to create a variant.

☞ QUESTION 16

Scheduling of planned order

There is this problem with scheduling: I have capacity in the WC (cat 0008) allocated in the views Scheduling and Capacities. But when I schedule planned order before saving it (MD11), the system issues the 'W' message:

"No capacity category has been maintained for scheduling in the work center specified in the operation".

The indicator "Capacity relevant to finite scheduling" is set in the capacity. All customizing for planned orders seems to be correct.

What could have possibly be wrong here?

I also customized shifts and set Grouping in Capacity, but system does not take into account the breaks between shifts, and considers only Standard Available capacity. What is causing this too?

✍ ANSWER

It may be the work center formulas. They must be enabled for capacity check. The planned order scheduling type (for your plant) must also have its own flag.

If you are interested in finite capacity check, take a look at the site:.http://digilander.libero.it/vietrim/index.html
For the second plant, activate scheduling with break indicator in tcode opu3.

☞ QUESTION **17**

Capacity Planning

When I run MRP, the system creates planned orders with backward planning logic. We find that it does not check the capacity available in the work centers and overloads it.

Is there a way where the system checks for the available capacity before scheduling it? That is, if the capacity in not available at a work center, it goes back and looks for next available slot and then schedule.

✍ ANSWER

U need to maintain the settings for production scheduler. In the production scheduler profile check the box "check available capacity "and "Finite scheduling ". Attach this to the production scheduler and then given this scheduler in the work scheduling view of the material master.

Now create an order and make the work center overload and see if this works.

In config for scheduling and capacity planning for planned order you will have to set it to load capacity.

Tnx - OPU5 select plnt and order type and whatever scheduling type you select tick cap. Reqmt
Also make sure you have the correct capacity category on the work center created for scheduling

MRP in SAP is based on Infinite scheduling, meaning that no capacity check is performed during MRP run.

If you want to do finite scheduling, you need to run it separately in another job. You can use CM40 to do so, but first you have to understand the logic and all configurations related to this functionality.

☞ Question 18

Components for lower level configurable not exploded

Higher level configurable material BIO2-N2_H has components COMP1, COMP2 and BIO2-N2_L (Lower level configurable). Configuration material BIO2-N2_L has components COMP3 and COMP4. BIO2-N2_L set up as Phantom (special procurement key 50). Selection conditions are assigned to components COMP1, COMP2 in the BOM for BIO2-N2_H and to components COMP3, COMP4 in the BOM for BIO2-N2_L. Configuration profiles for BIO2-N2_H and BIO2-N2_L have Planned/Prod order and Multi level indicator set and BOM application type PP01. BOMs for BIO2-N2_H and BIO2-N2_L are universal (BOM usage 3). When I go to CU50 for BIO2-N2_L, I select a characteristic value and go to result screen, I see the correct component selected. No problem there.

However, when I go to CU50 for BIO2-N2_H, I select a characteristic value for BIO2-N2_H and then select a characteristic value for BIO2-N2_L, then I see the component corresponding to the characteristic value of BIO2-N2_H in the results screen. But I do not see the component corresponding to the characteristic value of BIO2-N2_L in the results screen.

What could be the problem here? How can this be resolved?

✍ Answer

Try the sales order set. See if it works in CU50.

I am not sure why you enter the characteristic values

separately for B102-N2_H and B102-N2_L in the configuration Simulation.

When a characteristic value at header level is selected the same values have to be passed on to the lower levels also.

Make sure that you have attached the inheritance procedure to the configuration profile of lower level to enable passage of the values of the higher level configuration.

They can differ, which is precisely why you should write a constraint / procedure to copy values downward if you want them so. SAP will inherit downwards if it can, but not consistently.

Also, this should not affect the explosion at all (unless there are selection conditions on all components of the lower KMAT, and the characteristics are not passing down).

Selection conditions are assigned to all components of lower level KMAT and higher level KMAT except for the component lower level KMAT itself.

☞ QUESTION **19**

Local dependency

CU02 can change global dependency. Local dependencies can't be maintained centrally. This is the error we get.

How do I unlock the local locked dependency?

✍ ANSWER

Go to cu02, select the basic data and then change the status to release..

You can modify it at the same place where you had attached it in the bill of material or routing.

Instead of double-clicking on the dependency checkbox, go to dependencies>allocations, and then select "header."

☞ **QUESTION 20**

Reprint production order

I have already printed a production order.
When I am try to reprint it, the system is not allowing the command.

The error message is 'number BS-002'.

It says that 'reprint is not allowed and the user settings need to be checked'.

I have checked this forum and am not able to find the correct solution.

I have checked transaction code OKP8 & OPKP. However, I am not able to find which parameter controls the reprint of production and of production order in these transactions.

Were could the error have occurred and how can it be fixed?

✍ **ANSWER**

You can go to the production order and click on display status.

Click on tab Business process, check on reprint order, and then click on transaction analysis. This will indicate which status is blocking your printing. You can then go from there.

☞ **QUESTION 21**

Single Screen Confirmation

I need a confirmation in a single screen entry of production order TC (C011N).

How do I make the field "mandatory entry" even though it is being done in field selection for confirmation (co86) and it does not have an effect in Co11N?

✍ **ANSWER**

Base on Note 540734, you cannot do this in CO11N, but instead, you can do that in CO11.

You can do this using a screen variant with the use of transaction code "SHD0", where you can change a field property like: display only, invisible, and mandatory entry for a specific screen.

☞ QUESTION 22

With more than one component use LSMW for BOM

I use LSMW version 1.7.1

I want to know if it is possible to create the BOM (bill of material) with the LSMW transaction. I tried and succeeded to create the BOM with one component, but if I try to create the BOM with more than one component, the LSMW record will also give the possibility to more than one component.

Is there an explanation or methodology on how to use the LSMW in creating appropriate BOMS?

✍ ANSWER

I would suggest for you to go for BDC instead for less complications.

☞ **QUESTION 23**

Batch Management - Characteristics Report

We are using batch management. In the batch, we are entering some characteristics - say up to 10 characteristics. My problem is that I want to get all the characteristics used in a batch to appear as a report.

Say in batch 101, I am entering Roll no, diameter, width, etc. My report should be in such a way that if I enter the batch 101, a report has to be generated with all my characteristics used reflected.

Can I use a query for this purpose?

I have tried using the tables CABN, CABNNEW, etc. So far, nothing has worked according to purpose.

✍ **ANSWER**

Try to see BMBC. It might better serve your purpose.

☞ **QUESTION 24**

Configurable material/BOM

I would like to know about the configurable material/BOM. How should I start with it?

✍ **ANSWER**

Configurable materials have a bill of material that contains all components that are used in at least one variant. Likewise, the task list for the configurable material contains all operations that are used to manufacture at least one variant. By using the material configuration, only the components and operations that are required for one variant are selected.

Configurable materials are either created in a material type that allows the configuration (n the standard system, the material type KMAT) or they are given the indicator 'Configurable' in the material master record.

☞ QUESTION 25

Storage Resources

I am setting up a storage resources (linked to a storage location), with the purpose of being able to check the capacity of the storage location.

Inside the capacity header, we take capacity cat. 1 and input the available capacity unit as M2, minimum and maximum capacity.

After that, we check the available capacity by CM01 but found out that the available capacity is ALL ZEROS and can not display in M2 (only Hour).

I have been checking for a long time and started wondering if this function (concept) could actually work in SAP.

Is this possible in SAP? If yes, what should be the correct setup?

✍ ANSWER

I assume that you don't want to use WM to check the capacity of the storage location? WM would be better suited to your requirement.

I think using the work center will have a few problems. First, you need to have an operation that goes for the total time the finished goods are being stored. If you close the production order your storage requirement is removed. Second, storage requirements are dependent on volume and storage period of the finished goods, work centers would be based on a volume over time. For example, do you have 1 square meter x 5 days or 5 square meters x 1 day?

If you wanted a simple check on the volume of materials, you can maintain the volume in the material master and write a query to look at volumes for materials in stock or volume of finished goods still to be completed in the production orders. That would be a lot simpler to configure.

☞ QUESTION 26

Production Order Long Text

We have a requirement to populate the Production Order Long Text with the contents of Material Master Long text when the production order is created (CO01). This is for the header material or the material that is produced.

I did look at the user exit (PPCO0007) but was unable to find the correct field to populate the long text information.

I also created an order using a recording of co01. I could probably use the necessary text from a ztable. But I am not sure how to enter it in the production order.

Which field should be populated with this information?

Code:

```
FORM create_order_pp.

CLEAR: bdcdata.
REFRESH: bdcdata.

DATA: l_menge(13) TYPE c,
 l_datum(10) TYPE c,
 l_meins(3) TYPE c.

WRITE wa_krpos_order-menge_ausf
TO l_menge
LEFT-JUSTIFIED
DECIMALS 0.
WRITE sy-datum
```

TO l_datum.
SELECT SINGLE meins FROM mara
INTO l_meins
WHERE matnr EQ l_zzatnr.

PERFORM bdc_dynpro USING 'SAPLCOKO1' '0100'.
PERFORM bdc_field USING 'BDC_CURSOR'
    AFPOD-PWERK'.
PERFORM bdc_field USING 'BDC_OKCODE'
    '/00'.
PERFORM bdc_field USING 'CAUFVD-MATNR'
    l_zzatnr.
PERFORM bdc_field USING 'CAUFVD-WERKS'
    wa_krpos_order-werks.
PERFORM bdc_field USING 'AFPOD-PWERK'
    wa_krpos_order-werks.
PERFORM bdc_field USING 'AUFPAR-PP_AUFART'
    'zp01'.
PERFORM bdc_dynpro USING 'SAPLCOKO1' '0115'.
PERFORM bdc_field USING 'BDC_OKCODE'
    '/00'.
PERFORM bdc_field USING 'BDC_CURSOR'
    'CAUFVD-GLTRP'.
PERFORM bdc_field USING 'CAUFVD-GAMNG'
    l_menge.
PERFORM bdc_field USING 'CAUFVD-GMEIN'
    l_meins.
PERFORM bdc_field USING 'CAUFVD-GSTRP'
    l_datum.
PERFORM bdc_field USING 'CAUFVD-TERKZ'
    '1'.
PERFORM bdc_dynpro USING 'SAPLCOSD' '0310'.
PERFORM bdc_field USING 'BDC_OKCODE'
    '=OPT2'.
PERFORM bdc_dynpro USING 'SAPLCOKO1' '0115'.

PERFORM bdc_field USING 'BDC_OKCODE'
    '=BU'.
REFRESH: messtab.

CALL TRANSACTION 'CO01' USING bdcdata
    MODE 'E'
    UPDATE 'S'
    MESSAGES INTO messtab.

CLEAR: bdcdata.
REFRESH: bdcdata.

ENDFORM.

✍ ANSWER

Since you have already tried user-exit in enhancement PPCO0007, Use transaction COR2. Click on the pencil and in this field you can type in your long text.
You can also add some functions in file ZXCO1U06. There you can use some local functions to upload long-Text file, and I think you know function "Read Text" will be used.
You can transfer initial data from header_imp.

☞ **QUESTION 27**

Modified strategy 63

We are discussing merits/drawbacks of using strategy 63. We want to trigger the product assembly with sales order (and not with individual requirements for finished goods) but the fact is that customer order is usually too late in coming.

So we would like to differentiate sales orders to those which would trigger the assembly and those which would not.

Is there a possibility to do this?

✎ **ANSWER**

Try using a strategy 74 and mixed MRP 3. This will be more appropriate for your requirement.

☞ QUESTION 28

Demand Management

How can I upload a sales planning directly in DM through Xl file? Is there any mass processing available?

✍ ANSWER

Try the OMPL procedure.

☞ QUESTION 29

MRP RUN

How can I make MRP run in a GROSS Requirement planning strategy (11)?

What are the necessary steps to be taken?

✍ ANSWER

Basically, you should enter the independent requirement with BSF. The independent requirement drives the planned orders, without netting with current stocks and other receipt (that's gross requirement).

After which, you can execute MD02 or MD01 transaction.

Then, you have to maintain the mixed MRP to be 2 as well.

☞ QUESTION **30**

Capacity leveling - individual capacity (CM27)

When I move production order to its individual capacity with different scheduling date and scheduling time, the system doesn't change scheduling date and scheduling time of the production order to follow new scheduling.

Is this standard SAP work procedure or protocol?

If so, where can I set the appropriate configuration?

✍ ANSWER

You will have to check your MRP settings and believe it or not, you will have to set up conversion of planned order to production order in configuration. From there, you should specify that when planned order is converted to product order, it is converted as PP01 type. This should work for you.

For further insights on this subject, you can see some demo of finite capacity check in the site http://digilander.libero.it/vietrim/index.html.

☞ QUESTION 31

Capacity planning before actual planning

How do I formulate capacity planning before actual planning for a particular work center?

✍ ANSWER

There are several levels of capacity planning: for long-term planning (against a scenario), for planned order, and for a run schedule qty/prod order/proc order.

All these can happen if you setup the system correctly.

As for capacity planning for the work center, this is usually the result of the capacity planning mentioned before. If you want to do capacity leveling for a work center, then it is another story.

You can visit the site http://digilander.libero.it/vietrim/index. html for some demo about capacity check.

☞ QUESTION 32

Trouble with Scheduling

When I tried to schedule the planned order, the dates that the systems propose are too early, even if I increase the amount of the order.

I also tried another formula at the work center but it didn't help me either.

How can I propose specific dates in order to be in sync with the capacity of the work center?

✍ ANSWER

Standard works with finite capacity and basic dates are related to the production time of the material master. You can have different scheduled dates, proportionally to the quantity, etc. but not related to the effective load of the work center. Normally APO provides for this.

For further details, you can visit the site http://digilander. libero.it/vietrim/index.html for some demos about capacity check.

☞ **QUESTION 33**

Planned Orders and Capacity Evaluation

I have two problems with planned orders:

1. After MRP run, the planned orders created are not capacity checked. I have two materials A&B, planned orders Pa & Pb, and these two orders have operations 0010 in their MR(master recipe), in CM29 transaction - these two operations are scheduled with overlap! I have defined capacity check at the production scheduling profile, assigned them to the production scheduler and the material master (work scheduling view). Why is it still not looking at the available capacity?

2. I'm not able to dispatch these planned orders. I was told that planned orders cannot be dispatched. Why is this?

I want to check how my schedule looks before I convert them to process orders. Is this possible or not?

If yes, what should I do to at least schedule the planned orders manually to let the shop floor guys know how it looks ahead of time?

I'm at a client site and I need to tell them whether it is possible or not. I'm in 4.6C.

✍ **ANSWER**

You want to check the work center capacity availability during the planned order scheduling. Unfortunately, it's not possible. SAP works with infinite capacity. It can only give scheduled dates starting from the material routing or basic dates starting from the material master lead time. It does not provide for checking the real work center capacity.

I believe this can be done with APO though.

☞ **QUESTION 34**

Capacity Planning

Planned orders are generated based on the MRP run, but it does not give detailed schedule, unless order is scheduled on an individual basis.

Another problem is that once a planned order is scheduled for a particular work center, the system should not schedule another order, on the same timings which were scheduled on previous order.

Is it possible to generate planned order along with their detailed schedule on the MRP Run? If so, how is it done?

✍ **ANSWER**

When running the MRP for parameter "scheduling", select 2 (Lead time scheduling and capacity planning). This will schedule the planned order.

SAP R3 can only do infinite scheduling in which it assumes infinite capacity available at all work centers. If you want capacity constraints, then u need APO.

☞ QUESTION **35**

Work center basic data view

1. In work center basic data view, what are the meanings of various options of the 'Rule for Maintenance'?

2. What do we mean by performance efficiency rate?

I have the case for MRP below: 'Company 1000, Purchasing department create PO for parts A.

Design department create BOM using parts A1.

Actually, A1 is A just with some version change by the vendor.

While running MRP, A1 should be short of parts since there is no outstanding quantity defined for it.

Will there be any solution to allow the MRP to run for such a case, without users changing their PO?

✍ ANSWER

The rule for maintenance is based on how you want to control the input of the standard values in routing (for an operation involving the work center).

'Should / may not - generally means only a warning, "must" is mandatory.'

Performance efficiency rate is the rate that the work center is working at. 100% is normal working rate. If you alter the effectiveness of the work center, the standard times in capacity planning & costing are altered against the new rate.

If A and A1 have been maintained as two different material items (i.e. two different material number in SAP), then it is not feasible.

Instead, you can use auto-back flush to make the conversion between these two parts when receiving goods.

☞ QUESTION 36

Flag material for deletion

I flagged a material for deletion, but I can only get the warning message when I create a production order.

Even if we maintain message to E in O04C transaction for message number CO 732 (when creating production order), the user can still save the order.

Or, is there another transaction to be setup?

Usually i will use material status in material master to prevent production order creation for unwanted material.

But, I still have a doubt, why this deletion flag still can't prevent production order creation even if we already set the message to E.

I've tried to set the message ME 051 to E in OME0 transaction (for purchase order creation), and the system gives an error message thereby preventing the user from saving the PO.

If I want a error message of the deletion flag, what do I need to do? How can I check the configuration of the flag?

✍ ANSWER

What you have to do is to go to Transaction SE38 and make the proper modification of your Program LCOKOF1V where W732 shall be modified. Alternatively, go to Transaction OMS4 and set up the new Material Status Key where 'B' shall be maintained into the 'Production' Section. Assign this new

Material Status Key to your material master record.

I have found out an interesting thing that this kind of error could not take place not only in PP order but SD order as well (Message Number V1 406). Of course, from the MM point of view, such message as M7 127 can be set as 'E', this is not really the same in other modules.

'Use PP user' exists to error out for deleted flag items.

☞ QUESTION 37

COGI

I have two questions on COGI:

1. Is there any way to find the deleted records form COGI with out any processing involved?

2. In CO24, we get entries for material availability check, and then those entries vanish after the material is made available.

How can I get a list of the entries which were/are existing in CO24, just like for COGI in table - AFFWPRO.

✍ ANSWER

Response is given per number indicated in the question:

1. Standard SAP does not log the manually deleted entries of COGI.

If this log is required have a look at the SAP Note: 309050, only after implementation of the note. You can find the entries in AFFWPRO table with an update indicator as 'D'.

I will not recommend this as every entry in the COGI will get logged to this table requiring enormous database space. Even if it cleared through background processing, the entries will exist in this table with update indicator as U.

2. You can report error components from order in either RESB or AUFM. Try and check it.

☞ **QUESTION 38**

Decimal Places Error while defining Alternate UOM

While creating a material and defining its alternate UOM and its factor in decimal form, the system gives an error indicating that decimal places are not allowed.

We have a scenario in which 1 EA = 5.54 * 6.66 M, so we define 36.89 M2;

However it is not accepting decimal places. It gives this message:
'Message no. 00011'
How can this be resolved?

✍ **ANSWER**

Unfortunately, you should go for 1000 EA equal to 36890 M2.

You might also want to consider defining the decimal place for your UOM in Transaction CUNI.

☞ QUESTION **39**

Conversion of Planned Orders into PR for Product Order

When we run MD02 with settings: Processing key: NETCH;
>Create purchase requirement: 2 Purchase Required in opening period;
>For delivery schedules: 3 Schedule lines;
>Create MRP list: 1 MRP list;
>Planning mode: 1 Adapt planning data (normal mode);
>Scheduling: 1 Basic date will be determined for plan;
SAP generates purchase requirements for production orders and planned orders.

Is there a way so that SAP creates purchase requirements only for production orders and not for planned orders?

✍ ANSWER

The root cause of this problem was due to the fact that the 'Creation Requirement' indicator has been set as '2' instead of '1'. Therefore, the system always creates PR within the opening period and planned orders outside the opening period.

☞ **QUESTION 40**

Using Alternative BOMS

For production 1710598-001, I have 2 BOM set up, but I don't know how to make the work order pull the 2nd BOM. We are using 4.5b.

Do you know how to make a work order pull an alternative BOM?

✍ **ANSWER**

There are several ways to select alternate BOMs:

1. Use validity dates on the BOM header.

2. Use lot sizing on the BOM.

3. Set up production versions in the material master so that alt 2 is selected instead of alt 1.

☞ QUESTION 41

Pricing determination for Activity Type

I have to create a new activity type and a cost center and then assign it in my work center. So I have created a new, GL account to my controlling area Cost Center as follows:

>Primary and Secondary cost elements
>Activity type
>Activity type – Pricing Plan

With this new activity type and cost center, I run through my SFC cycle during Order Confirmation and I am getting an Error message of:

"No price could be determined for object activity type Controlling area/Cost center/Activity type - *** / **** / **** "

When coming back an error box appears saying:

"Error determining actual cost for order ****** "

How can I locate the mistake and rectify it?

I have also maintained Activity price using Transaction - KP26, even then the same problem with the same error message appears.

How can I also confirm the Production Order?

✍ ANSWER

If you already maintain activity price using Transaction -

KP26 for the current period & Year -for the combination of Cost center/Activity type, try checking the configuration in OPL1 to check the CO version you have used.

Another item to check is whether the difference in defining unit of measurement in parameters defined for standard value key in PP customizing and UOM defined for activity by the Controlling Consultant.

☞ QUESTION **42**

Maximum number of group counters in Routing Group

SAP is telling 'to create maximum 10 counters for one routing group'.

What will happen if I create more than 10?
Is this logic applicable for all types of routings in SAP?

✍ ANSWER

This is incorrect. You can have as many counters as you like for a routing number, including an alpha and alphanumeric notations.

To my knowledge, there is no restriction. It is a 2 length character field, so it can accept numeric till 99, alpha numeric and 2 character numeric.

☞ QUESTION 43

MTO or MTS?

1. As company policy, we can only generate production orders based on the real sales orders, not rolling forecast. But our purchasing needs to run component MRP based on the rolling forecast. It's because our order lead time is short, but material purchasing lead time is long. How do I reconcile this kind of MRP strategy?

2. Our production mode is MTO. My question is: if we go to MTO solutions in SAP, can we generate production order from sales orders directly and not thru MRP program? And if production order bound with specified sales order, how do we switch inventory to other sales order at the time of shipment if the customer has an urgent request?

3. Our top level, finished goods level is MTO, the following semi-finished and raw material level is MTS. So can we put forecast requirements on the semi-finished level instead of finished goods level?

✍ ANSWER

Responses are given according to question numbers:
1. You can still use lot-for-lot in MTS, and MRP does not have to automatically convert planned orders. Furthermore, any strategy that can utilize long-term planning should allow you to plan and procure the components without forcing you to convert planned orders into production orders.

    However, it is possible to move from one order to another with the correct chain of inventory movements. Because

MTO typically is non-valuated and settled against the sales order, you will have a slew of costing concerns to watch.

2. Yes, you can tie a planned or an assembly order to a sales order through the requirements class. If you have a high volume and need to switch from one order to another, MTS makes a whole lot more sense. MTS does not mean you have to stock up -- you can still make as needed based on MRP driving the demand. This will give you simplified planning and inventory management.

3. Sure, why not? The dependent requirements from the MTO order will consume the plan for the MTS assemblies.

☞ QUESTION 44

Auto selection of Routing at Production order creation

I do have multiple routings (production versions) for a finished product. The information is flowing from sales order (MTO scenario). My requirement is for the system to select the appropriate routing automatically and then create the production order automatically.

Is there any program or user exit I can use?
How can it be automated?

✍ ANSWER

Automatic creation of production order is possible with assembly to order strategy.

☞ **QUESTION 45**

Production Version and the document year 2006

Our Environment is SAP R/3 4.6c.

I keep getting the message "Production version not extended for the document year 2006". I have checked and the material production version has been extended in MRP view 4. What could be wrong here?

✍ **ANSWER**

Check the validity period of the production version you are using. The validity may be ending 31/12/2005. You can use transaction C223 OR MM02 to change this validity.

☞ **QUESTION 46**

Capacity planning in PP

Can anybody help in providing me step by step configuration settings for capacity planning?

✍ **ANSWER**

You can do this configuration:

OPCF – Define UM
OP7B – Parameter of Measure -> Energy, Volume, etc.
O7CM – Define Matrix values to TCode- CR01 to CR03
OPCN – Matrix – Delivery Time
OP4A – Define Shift program
OPCR and OPCS – Define Formula (Example Overhead)
OPJP – Define programming class
OPCH – Define Group Production control

☞ QUESTION **47**

Routing query

Table PLPO and PLKO isn't enough to fulfill the routing query report.

What other table for material or work center can I use?

✍ ANSWER

You can use the s022 table. Also, in addition to PLPO and PLKO, use MAPL.

☞ QUESTION 48

Relevance of ownership of material

Scenario 1: One material was received under a different material code.

For maintaining secrecy of the final product, raw materials are issued to the production centers with code. For example: same raw material is issued to the different production center with a different material code. While collecting the final product (which is received under same code as the raw material) all the stocks are arriving with a different name. There are about 50 such codes for each material.

This final products from production centers then undergo processing and treatment and finally packed under a Marketing Code variety. The stock position should be available at any stage with all quality parameters for all the codes.

Important Note: Throughout the lifecycle of the product, quality parameters are measured at different stages and should be traceable from any stage.

Scenario 2: Material is taken into stock only after certain processing and quality check thereafter.

Raw material is received from the vendor and processed in either own plant or leased plant. After processing, if the product meets the quality parameters, only then is the stock taken into account and payment is made to the vendor. Until that time, the stock ownership is the vendor's only. Without ownership of the material, can it be consumed in a Production/Process Order?

Requirement: The stock position should be available at any stage with all quality parameters.

✍ ANSWER

Actually, if the stock is in the vendor consignment stock, it is possible to issue to production orders from this stock type.

Once you issued out your vendor consigned stock to your order, you did actually consume this stock. For example, the stock ownership has been transferred to you (through the generation of accounting document) who are not meeting the original business requirement.

☞ QUESTION **49**

Partial Reversal of Production Order

Is there a way in SAP wherein we can reverse partial quantities of previously confirmed production order?

✍ ANSWER

You can reverse the entire confirmation (CO13), and then re-input the correct confirmation. I do not know of a way (except for a table hack!) of amending a confirmation.

☞ QUESTION **50**

Unable to schedule Production Order on Jan 2 /06

Our US Plant Factory Calendar is a working day for January 2, 2006 and assigning to plant V-T001W also went well.

However, we are unable to schedule any Production order for January 02 and it moves either to December 31, 2005 or January 3, 2006. The Mexico plant worked fined with the schedule date and the only problem is with the US plants.

How can we locate the problem and how do we fix this?

✍ ANSWER

January 2, 2006 is the New Year's holiday. Therefore, I would start by looking at the factory calendar – that is the factory calendar assigned to the Work center involved in the Production order.

Check it in the capacity header of the Work Center.

☞ QUESTION 51

COPY BOM from Production to costing

We have implemented a few months ago a scrap factor in our BOM to have a better planning structure. However, the Finance department is now requiring us to remove it. They (Finance) don't want to put costing to it.

How can we have costing without creating a new BOM?

If we need to create a new Costing BOM, is there a way to create those en masse?

How do we keep it in sync if the production BOM change?

Is there any standard program?

✍ ANSWER

I think BDC will be the best option for your situation.

You need one BDC to copy the existing BOM and make a new BOM with costing as usage.

Another option is to remove the Scrap definition of the BOM.

☞ QUESTION **52**

Pegged Requirements

Can someone please explain to me the meaning of pegged requirements?

✍ ANSWER

Pegged requirements is defined as a requirement which shows the next level parent item (or customer order) as the source of the demand, (i.e. by using the where-used capability from the BOM).

☞ QUESTION 53

ATP check problem

We want to use the ATP check for production order and set up a background job for ATP check each day just after the MRP total run.

After we checked the result, we found that there was some misunderstanding.

The system always gives committed and confirmed quantity base on production creation date and not with the requirement date.

Is there some setting related with that? If so, how can I change the ATP check with the component requirement date?

✍ ANSWER

One suggestion - create multiple jobs of PPIO_ENTRY, each one with different relative date selection criteria. It means that the first job run for all orders will have a start date in the past. Then the next job would be all orders with a start date of today, etc.

This could work depending on your lead times and volumes.

The system is just grouping them - all sorted by production order number, which, in effect is the same as the creation date.

☞ QUESTION 54

Reorder Point for FERT

I want to know if it is possible to configure the Reorder Point for materials FERT, although the Planned Order has to be created for another Company.

What happens if it is a Special procurement scenario? Can we not suggest "juliaquercia" to go for Stock transfer Special procurement key so that his requirement of creating a demand for another plant in a different company code will be met?

✍ ANSWER

For the first questions, the answer is no. It is not feasible as the MRP run is made at the plant level of a certain company code.

For the second question, I would be much doubtful if the Special Procurement Type can be the right solution. The requirement is that once it is running MRP at one plant, the system will generate the planned order at the other plant. In fact, the special procurement type is only enabling you to generate the stock transfer requisition at the other plant which will then be converted into STO (Stock Transport Order).

☞ **QUESTION 55**

Production Order

Is there any transaction available to see all production orders completed in the last few months?

✍ **ANSWER**

Try the TCode "COOIS". CO28 could also prove helpful.

☞ QUESTION 56

Problem with automatic scrap

I would like to ask for your help about an issue we are faced regarding automatic scrap. I have read some topics about automatic scrap, tried to apply the proposed solutions and I wonder if I have the appropriate customizing to use it.

I declare production using MFBF, repetitive manufacturing, back flush type is "assembly back flush".

I have planned order but I don't put it in the MFBF transaction to declare my production (repetitive manufacturing).

I have put a component scrap percentage in the BOM item detail (10%).

In my planned order I get a required quantity that includes the scrap quantity (thus 110%). If I run my MRP, the required quantity is also 110% but when I declare my production I only back flush 100% (movement code 261) and nothing is scrapped (I expected movement 551 or something like that).

Is there something I missed in the material master data of the component or on the REM profile I use on the finished goods?

✍ ANSWER

Try to maintain a component scrap in rate routing and go from there.

☞ **QUESTION 57**

Make Versus Buy

We have a situation where a material we manufacture is to be purchased from 1st June 2006. MRP is creating planned order today but we would like to create planned orders till 31 May 2006 and requisition after that.

Is this possible?

We converted planned order to requisitions beyond 1st June 2006 to support production then but the requisitions are getting pegged to orders before 1st June 2006.

We are on 4.7 release of R3.

How do we go about resolving this issue?

✍ **ANSWER**

One of the solutions is to change the Procurement Type from 'E' into 'F'. This will enable the generation of purchase requisitions instead of planned orders.

Changing the procurement type will help, but it might also create problems when currently using the material. This might also affect the costing of this material.

Another option is to use quota arrangements where you source via production version (if being used) up until 31 May 2006, and source via source list (PIR) after that date.

If they are all valuated differently and you would like to keep such difference, then you can think of using the split valuation functionality.

☞ **QUESTION 58**

Capacity Planning-PP

This is regarding capacity planning in discrete manufacturing. I want to view capacity requirement generated against sales order (Production orders against a particular sales order). Simultaneously, it should show the status of work center

(whether work center is overloaded & if not, what is the remaining available capacity).

Is this possible? If so, how can this be accomplished?

✍ **ANSWER**

It is possible. Try using TCode CM50.

☞ QUESTION 59

Capacity Planning

Scenario:

Machine 1: 300kg / 3 hours

No. of Shifts: 2 shifts / 8 hours per shift

How can you prevent planning from creating order if 5 PO's are already scheduled in Machine 1, which is equal to 15 hours?

Can you please give me a step by step procedure in setting the solution?

✍ ANSWER

You define the formula like (SAP_09 * SAP_02 / SAP_08). Whenever you create the PO, the order quantity is taken and calculated how much time is taken for this operation under the work center.

In your case, Machine 1 can produced 100 Kg / h. Suppose you create the PO for 150 Kg. you applied these formula 150* 1/ 100 = 1.5 Hr like 1hr 30 Min.

You can have the system perform a capacity check upon order creation/release by making the appropriate settings in configuration (T-code OPJK).

Further, you really need to balance capacity in a two step process. First, orders are created (planned, process, production, etc.) either manually or via MRP. Next, you need to level capacity, i.e., do finite scheduling on each of your resources (CM29 for process, CM21 for discrete). Advanced planning systems like APO can do this in one step, but R/3 requires it be done in two.

☞ QUESTION **60**

Select order in capacity leveling

When I do dispatching to the work center, it has an individual capacity = 2. Then SAP will show 2 production orders on the work center line at the same schedule time and show a green line. The question is how to select the below order, because every time I click the system, it will select the front production order.

How do I resolve this?

✍ **ANSWER**

There are several overall profiles you can use via CM25.

You need to select one that has an order view of the data as well (or instead) of a resource view.

If you wish to create your own profile, the ability to have overlapping orders show up parallel to one another instead of appearing overlaid when viewed against the same resource. This is also configurable.

☞ QUESTION 61

Storage Capacity Planning

Is it possible to plan capacity of storage?

For example:

Material being produced is stored in tanks whose storage capacity is limited. I need to find out the storage volume required for the production.

I created resource with resource category of processing unit/storage resource. In this resource, I created capacity category Warehouse + procurement unit. I entered relevant data in the section Available capacity as volume/quantity. I created the relevant recipe for the material as well.

When I check for the capacity requirements generated by the system, I get capacity requirements only in hours where as I require it to be in volume.

I have defined parameter with dimension as Volume and UoM as M3 (Cubic meter). I have also defined the formula.

In capacity data, system only takes data from the section 'Standard Available capacity'. Here, I cannot enter data with UoM as M3. The system allows only UoM with dimension of time.

The data entered in the section 'Available capacity as volume/ quantity' is not being referred.

Am I still missing something?

✍ Answer

Check your definition of your formula parameters for the unit of measure you want to calculate the capacity in. That may be causing some confusion within earlier configurations.

☞ **QUESTION 62**

Capacity Requirements

Can someone tell me the table where the Capacity Requirements (Past and Future) per capacity / Work Center are stored?

✍ **ANSWER**

For the current capacity requirements try the following tables:

KAKO - Capacity Header Segment
KBED - Capacity Requirements Records
CRCA - Work Center Capacity Header
CRHD - Work Center Header

☞ QUESTION **63**

Detailed Scheduling in Planned Order

When using detailed scheduling and capacity planning, the system is not automatically providing timings to the operations in the planned orders generated at MRP Run. However, when in change mode of any planned orders, scheduling is possible of operations or work centers, when using scheduling is run.

Is it possible that this planning is done at MRP Run, rather than by going onto individual planned orders and executing scheduling or rescheduling?

✍ **ANSWER**

Better check your MRP parameters and in the parameters for capacity and scheduling (i think from memory, you have to choose 2).

☞ QUESTION **64**

BOMs not created in new plant

I have created a new plant and attached the same to one company code which is already available in the system. Then I've created Materials too (ROH, HALB and FERT).

My problem is, while creating BOM the error message is material type (ROH, HALB and FERT) is not maintained for item category "L" i.e. stock item. It is not allowing to create BOM with material ROH/ HALB/ FERT.

(But BOMs are created in system defined plants).

✍ ANSWER

You problem is very simple. After creating the plant, you need to setup the valuation of every material type for the valuation area. Example, for a material type in a valuation area how it should be accounted, whether in terms of QTY or Value or both.

Do this configuration in OMS2.

☞ QUESTION 65

Transfer planning to demand management

We have created sales forecast using flexible SOP. Now, while we are trying to transfer these details to demand planning using MD90, the system gives an error that currently displayed data will not be transferred. We are using customized info structure with consistent planning. I am able to do the same with info structure with level by level planning.

Can anyone please let me know how to transfer production forecast from SOP to Demand Planning – specifically, where info structure with consistent planning is used?

✍ ANSWER

By using mass processing functionality in SOP by creating transfer profiles and activities we can transfer the data to Demand management.

Using SOP method, demand can be transferred like direct pir method by using md87, md78.

☞ QUESTION 66

Recipe with materials assignment with different BOMs

I am creating a recipe with material assignment with three finished products as the routing is same but BOMs are different. How do I assign different BOMs in same recipe for different FERTs? Is it possible or shall I create a separate recipe for all products?

✍ ANSWER

You will need to create a production version and link the different Alternative BOMs and recipes.

☞ **QUESTION 67**

Field PLPOD-LTXA2 in Routing

I want to enter some quality check texts required for operations in the routing besides the operation short text. In PLPOD table of Routing, two fields LTXA1 & LTXA2 are available but only LTXA1 (short text) is available for input.

I want to make LTXA2 field in routing for input as LTXA1. Is this possible?

✍ **ANSWER**

Yes it is possible. In the long text for the operation, enter text in the second line. This will be updated in the PLPO-LTXA2 field.

☞ QUESTION 68

MRP requirements

I am new to PP. After MRP run I want to see the requirements. Where do I have to check for requirements? I saw MD04 and MD05, which one do I have to consider?

What is the difference between MD04 and MD05?

✍ ANSWER

MD05 is a static list which shows the details of the last run MRP for the combination of material and plant.

Meanwhile, MD04 is a dynamic list which gives you the Current Stock/Requirements list. This list gives you an update after considering the changes which are done after the MRP run also.

☞ QUESTION 69

Where to find the deleted order

Where or from which table I can find the deleted production?

✍ ANSWER

If the process order is archived after setting Deletion Indicator, then you will be able to find it using transaction CO78. Go for retrieval of data.

If archiving is not done, I am afraid you won't be able to see the record.

☞ QUESTION **70**

Close production order with external purchase order

I want to close my production order which has an external purchase order. Even if I do final goods receipt and final invoice for this purchase order and the final GR & final IR indicator both have been flagged, I still can not close the production order.

System error message is:

CO434
Production order XXXXXXXX purchase order XXXXX still exists.

Is it a program error?

✍ ANSWER

Check SAP notes 650829 & 773397.

☞ QUESTION 71

Customer requirements allocation issue (TCode MD73)

Does the phrase "allocation of customer independent requirements" mean assignment of the customer requirements to the independent requirements versions? Is that the consumption of planned independent requirements by customer independent requirements?

If so, what are the independent requirements versions used for? Is it just to classify the requirements?

✍ ANSWER

In LTP, you can use another version number. It is also an inactive version.

☞ QUESTION **72**

Canceling order confirmation

I encountered a problem on cancelling order confirmation.

The error message indicated is:

"Future change records for background processing exist for order 500232288".

I followed the help index to run the program CORUPROC. But it wasn't very helpful. Then I checked the back flushing via transaction CO1P and found there are two parts that were not issued. However, I can not found any error via transaction COGI.

What is the problem here and how can this be resolved?

✍ ANSWER

The mechanism in confirmation of production order is done after we post the records. The background job will do the posting asynchronously, meaning return the screen to user to do something else, while still posting the data. You can control whether it's online or in a background job depending on configuration OPKC. The program CORUPROC is the background program that is supposed to do the posting.

If we choose background, it improves the performance of the dialog for the users. After a while, the background job completes posting the data from confirmation. Then, you can cancel your confirmation.

If you opt immediately after posting, the system will be bogged down until the posting is done. If you have a lot of components to back flush, I would not recommend you to do it on-line.

☞ **QUESTION 73**

Material creation problem

I have created a new plant & material component.

I have to change the material requirement in MRP 4 view. But when I try to opt for collective requirement only, I get the error:

"Only individual planning possible (No quantity based inventory management)".

How do I correct the error?

✍ **ANSWER**

For the material type of the material you are using to change the Individual and Collective requirements, the valuation is not defined for Quantity and Value.

Better redefine using Customizing Transaction OMS2 for the material type and for the Plant combination as well.

☞ QUESTION 74

BOM creation problem

I have created a new plant & material in a new plant location. While creating BOM in new plant, it gives me the error:

"Material type ROH with item category L (Plant 9901)"

"Material type HALB with item category L (Plant 9901)"

"Material type FER with item category L (Plant 9901)"

How can this be resolved?

✍ ANSWER

Complete your valuation settings for the material type for the new plant in Customizing transaction OMS2.

☞ QUESTION **75**

Production Scenario -Sticker Industry

I am involved with an implementation project at a sticker manufacturing plant. The scenario here is a little different from the usual scenarios we come across in a discrete industry. I will explain the process.

The stickers are produced by various 8/9 processes like screen printing, curing, lamination, cutting etc. The final product is an individual sticker but this sticker is produced as a part of layout sheet until the final stamping out operation and later on two operations are done on an individual sticker.

The issue here is, the layout sheet (by design) is not a separate sheet for different sticker types (final products) but it is a combination of the different stickers of various shapes and sizes. This is done to reduce the scrap percentage of the sheets.

The process is a batch managed process where various processes are carried out on the sheet.

The client wants to track the WIP for the individual stickers (which are part of the layout sheet) at all the stages. The planning is done for the final product sticker. There are multiple layout sheets available for a single product. The layout is selected based on the orders on hand and the current inventory of the stickers on the layout.

I want to understand how one should create a Bill of Material and the production orders. How can we track the individual stickers in WIP?

✍ ANSWER

First of all, I suggest that you take a look at the apparel industry solution and best practices, as this problem occurs there too.

Second, there may be more than one way to define the bill of materials, but no one is perfect for all the BOM uses (e.g. MRP planning, costing, etc.).

The first option would be to choose a leading sticker type for each sheet, which will then become the BOM header, and the rest of the sticker types on the same sheet would be by products. This option has the potential to work well with WIP (production orders), but may pose some issues in costing and planning.

The second option would be to have a separate BOM for each sticker type (as BOM header), and have a different material number for each sheet layout type. In this kind of BOM, define the resulting quantity ratio between the sticker and sheet, and define all other possible sheets that include the same sticker as alternative items (for the cases when you use a different sheet layout type). This option is not perfect either, since it still raises yet different issues regarding planning and costing. If there's a wrong calculation of the number of required sheets, it needs to be rectified (maybe using some additional functionality that may have to be developed). The advantage here is that you can get a more natural trace of the sheets batches in WIP.

You can try the various options and apply whichever works best for your situation.

☞ QUESTION **76**

Strategy 11

Strategy 11 is not activating properly. I also tried the MRP 3 view but I am unable to access it.

I would like to understand all the procedures involved to correct the situation. Can the process be explained in detail?

✒ ANSWER

Strategy group 11 will not take off from the current stock as the positive quantity in MRP calculation.

You have to set strategy group to 11 and mix MRP to 2, availability check to 02, and sales item category to NORM. This information is contained in the SAP help file. You may want to take a look at the scenarios first before you actually spend time in testing it.

☞ **QUESTION 77**

By-products & Co-products

What settings in BOM / Material Master distinguish a Co-product from a By-product?

✍ **ANSWER**

During the creation of Material Master, one has to define material type and material number. Both series are unique for each and every material type that designates what type of material is a Co-Product or a By-product.

We did not have to use the material type to separate from co-, and by-product.

The main difference is co-product can run cost estimates and by-product does not have to run cost estimates.

The co-product is flagged in MRP view and also the proportional factor of the costs (in Joint Production pushbutton; so-called disproportional factor) to split the costs between main and co-product. You also have to maintain the co-product flag in the BOM items as well.

Both by-, and co-product are maintained as negative quantity in BOM.

☞ QUESTION 78

Strategy Options

I'm looking for a strategy which would function this way:

- Component should be produced ahead, based on independent requirement for this component (component is used in many different finished products).

- Assembly of finished product shouldn't start with sales order, because that would be too late. Instead, it should be based on independent requirement of finished products.

I've looked into strategy 50/52, 60/62, but the assembly is triggered here by the sales order.

In reference to the above requirements, what strategy would pose as the best option to take?

✍ ANSWER

Your finished goods are make-to-stock with final assembly. Therefore, you should opt for strategy 10, or 40.

Your component is based on independent requirement. Therefore, you should choose 70 planning at the assembly level.

☞ QUESTION 79

Lead time off set

LTP and operative MRP are sharing the same BOM. When I set the lead time off in BOM, I tried to get all the component requirements to fall into the same month, instead it went in operative MRP and I don't want that.

How do I get out of this?

✍ ANSWER

I don't think that you can use lead time offset to do so.

Try using the lot size key for long-term lot size (configuration OMI4) and use scheduling to be 2 (period end = delivery date). You might also want to disable lead-time scheduling as well.

If your long-term period is falling short, you may want to use gross lot size maintenance in planning scenario instead. It will override what is maintained in material master. The only problem is the rounding value will not be taken into account.

☞ QUESTION 80

Super BOM

What is a Super BOM?

How do I use it & how are settings done in SAP?

✍ ANSWER

Super BOM is where the product is possible to produce with different features by combining various components available in the BOM.

The selection of the component from the BOM for the production order will be based on the configuration of the product in the sale order.

The configuration of the Product in the sale order drives the selection of the component based on Dependency, Selection conditions, preconditions procedures etc. which are in turn, defined.

The bill of material (BOM) of a configurable material contains all the components that are required to manufacture the material. The BOM contains components that are only used in specific variants (variant parts), as well as components that are used in all variants (non-variable parts).

This is why BOMs for configurable materials are known as Super BOMs.

☞ QUESTION 81

Re-Scheduling

I have one problem regarding scheduling.

Suppose I have one BOM with the following specs:

    X-header
    Y- Assembly
    Z-raw

I have created PIR for X and ran the MRP. If opening date is in the past for Y is shown then how should I reschedule the order and how should I block the production order confirmation for X when material shortage exist (i.e. user should know the material is not available at the start date of X)?

✍ ANSWER

Define check control to reject release when missing parts exists for the order - Transaction OPJK. Confirmation will be allowed only for released status orders.

☞ QUESTION 82

Common problems while Running MRP

I am quoting some common problems which I encountered during the MRP run.

I have created PIR for finished material and while running MRP (MD02), the dependent requirement for the raw material was shown as 1-; I don't know what the problem is. How do I determine where I went wrong and how do I correct the error?

✍ ANSWER

Your problem seems to be in understanding how to read the Stock/requirement list (MD04) or MRP list (MD05).

The quantity column denotes Quantity received or Quantity required. Depending on the relevant MRP element, this value specifies either the quantity received or the quantity required.

In your case this is quantity received 1- as it is an issue element (reservation-dependent requirement).

☞ **QUESTION 83**

Target cost in process order

Can anybody tell how to get the target cost in cost analysis of process order?

Is there any setting in configuration or master data which I am missing?

✍ **ANSWER**

Here are some pointers you need to go over:

1. Target cost version needs to be setup in OKV6 transaction for the controlling area you are using.

2. There has been some GR for the order.

3. Variance is calculated for the order.

4. Based on the definition of the Target cost version - Standard cost estimate exists for the product.

☞ **QUESTION 84**

BOM at date in the past

Is there any way of getting the BOM for material in the past? I know function CS_BOM_EXPL_MAT_V2 has the date input parameter, but it does not seem to work properly. I changed the material on one of the component lines of a BOM and then ran the above function with yesterdays date, and it returned the new material I had entered today. I deleted the component line and then re-created it with a new material and when I run the above function for yesterday, the component I deleted does not appear and the new component only appears when I run it with today's date.

I am currently working on 4.6C.

How can I fix this issue?

✍ **ANSWER**

Do you use ECN? If not, then it is not possible to keep change history of BOM.

If you only need to interrogate one BOM at a time, run transaction CS03 without any valid-from and valid-to dates (or with dates over the date range you are after). This will display some of the changes against each item, regardless of whether ECM was used or not. If you require changes to the Header or need more detailed info regarding the changes made, then transaction CM80 might help.

☞ QUESTION **85**

Packing of by-products

My client wants to pack waste or byproducts in bales or in cartons - that is not in equal quantity, and wants to upload in SAP Stock. After which they want to sell the product.

Can any one help me how to configure in SAP the uploading of the material?

Should it be shown in MMBE in bale wise or lot wise?

✍ ANSWER

Use the appropriate handling unit management by which you can resolve the above mentioned concerns.

Maintain alternate unit of measure as a packing unit by maintaining relation with Base unit of measure of material and upload the quantity in the system using MB1C with mvt type 561 .

☞ QUESTION **86**

Object dependencies to calculate labor hours

I wanted to set up object dependencies to calculate labor hours based on the characteristic values of characteristic ' Model', ' BF', and ' MB'.

I used the following procedure:

$SELF.LABOUR = MDATA $SELF. + 2 IF Model eq '1020'

To add, for example, 2 hours to the equation.

However, I calculated that I need to create 500 object dependencies to cover all possible combinations. Is there any other way to calculate the total of labor time based on characteristic values assigned in the sales order? Can I put the characteristic values in a table and 'tell' SAP to calculate the sum of the characteristic values?

Example:

BF MB Total labor time
Model:
1010 1 2 3
1020 2 2 4
1030 0, 5 1 1, 5

✍ ANSWER

The answer is actually quite simple:

BF MB Total labor time
Model:
1010 1 2 3
1020 2 2 4
1030 0, 5 1 1, 5

To continue the equation:

$SELF.LABOUR = MDATA $SELF. LABOUR+ 1 IF Model eq
'1010'
SELF.LABOUR = $SELF. LABOUR+ 2 IF Model eq '1020'
SELF.LABOUR = $SELF. LABOUR+ 0.5 IF Model eq '1030'

Try it and have a dry run.

You can use a variant table. You can put everything in
one procedure, as described above, but you will still have
500 lines. If you use a table, you can at least make this
maintainable by a user.

You can also use variant functions, if you have a simple
enough formula.

☞ Q**UESTION** 87

Product Number Range

I'm looking for information for an internal number range.

How can we segment a number range based on the product type:

Say, for liquid 1000000 to 3999999;
For solid 4000000 to 6999999;
For gas 7000000 to 9999999;

Can User exists or can custom development help to resolve this?

Will a number range (Internal number) allocation for Recipe Group be made possible?

✍ A**NSWER**

I assume you mean production order number since material number range can basically vary by material type already.

What you can do is use MRP Group as the way to default the production order type. You can also default MRP group by MRP type.

The individual conversion of each planned order will use this order type. However, if you use CO41, the problem will recognize the last order type in parameter ID "AAT". That will override the default setting in the MRP group.

You can also resolve this by creating a field exit for CO41 tcode not to take the parameter AAT.

For the second question, unfortunately it is not possible. I don't think there is a user exit for it.

One way is to configure the number range to turn off the internal number and having only an external number range that are in your list.

Then user just has to enter the recipe group manually by copying the material number to the recipe group.

Check your detail requirement whether this will work or not.

☞ **QUESTION 88**

Order Confirmation - Act Labor vs. Standard Labor

During processing of the CO11N (Confirmation), I entered the actual labor and machine hours. However, the Standard goes through the General Ledger.

What I really need to know is the actual figures entered when processing the confirmation.

Is there a report I can download out of SAP that can give me both, either in one report or in separate reports?

✍ **ANSWER**

Check for COOIS> Select Operations in the top field and in the results screen change you can bring in the actual hours. This gives you the total confirmed hours for an operation.

If you want to see each individual confirmation you need to look at table AFRU.

You can also check the AFVV table with routing operation number and counter. This you will get from kbed table for a particular work center.

☞ QUESTION 89

Sample material issue against production order

In my scenario, against a production order, sample FERT material is issued and after completion of that production order, that sample FERT material is again received.

For example:

There is one FERT material created through some other production cycle.

For our main production cycle, this sample actually moves through the production line along with the production order. Throughout the production cycle, this sample is physically out of the storage location and only after completion of that production cycle does this sample (FERT) goes back to its storage location.

The Client needs to record the movement of the sample because all samples remain accumulated in the sample storage location.

How do I take that FERT sample material in my BOM component? After which, if I get it issued as my component, how can I do GR after production order completion?

✍ ANSWER

Let me consider your final product as X - Maintain co-product indicator in the MRP2 View.

Maintain co-product indicator for Sample (Fert) in the MRP2 view,

Now, you can add Sample as two line items in the BOM of X, one with positive quantity and another with negative quantity.

In the component details of the negative quantity line item, activate the Co-Product indicator.

This should solve your problem. Now you can Issue Sample and also receive sample.

On the costing part you need to maintain equivalence number for material X with respect to Sample (Fert).

☞ QUESTION 90

Table T457C

I don't know the usage of maintaining table T457C. The item in the table includes the following fields:

> >Transact Group
> >MRP element individual
> >Status
> >Transaction code
> >Initial screen
> >Parameter ID
> >Field name

What is the function of each field?

✍ ANSWER

This table is mainly used for default navigation in stock requirement list and MRP lists. As far as I know, there is no direct customizing for this table.

If you want to change the button, say, double click on PR show push button for PR change, PR release, e.g., you can configure this using navigation profile (Production -> Material Requirement Planning -> Evaluation -> Define navigation profiles).

MRP Element is the type of element shown in stock requirement list such as production order (FE), PR (BA), sales order (VC).

☞ QUESTION 91

Mass change base quantity of BOMs and routing

I have 2 work centers and both their base quantity is 1000.

Is it possible to have a mass change (of BOMs and routing) with this quantity on 994?

✍ ANSWER

You could write a batch input routine. Coordinate this with your development /abap team.

☞ **QUESTION 92**

Trouble with dates of production

I am currently using Repetitive manufacturing and I encountered problems when I used the Planification Table (MF50). When I tried to assign an amount to a line production, a message appears in the button of the screen:

"No production dates for material 1000002, version 0003, production line MM-01-SD

The planned order has no production dates for the combination of material, production version and production line you specified.

This may be as a result of the following, for example:

The planned order was scheduled but not using the production line you selected. (The production line is determined by the production version you entered in a planned order.)"

I did everything that they mentioned. I also checked all the master information like material version, routings, and work centers. In customizing, I checked in CRP (Capacity Planning) for the Plant but nothing looks unusual.

✍ **ANSWER**

Check if you have provided the correct entries in the production line (Critical Work center) in the production version 003.

☞ QUESTION 93

Quantity delivered in production order screen shows zero

We have a few production orders where the final confirmation has been done and full delivery has been made. However, the quantity delivered field in the production order screen shows zero. Why is that happening?

✍ ANSWER

Check the status if it is DLV. If not, check the COGI transaction, this transaction displays the good movement errors. Give the plant and the order number and check for 101 MVT type line item.

☞ QUESTION 94

Labor characteristic in Variant Configuration

I use a reference characteristic to calculate labor in procedures that are allocated to the operation on the master routing. This works fine. But now, I want to use this total value for another purpose in a constraint. However, it doesn't seem to see the calculated value. How can I make this value available to a constraint or procedure located on the configuration profile?

✍ ANSWER

If the calculation of the labor value occurs on the profile, just place it in sequence prior to the procedure where you wish to use the result. This may not be possible with a constraint, depending on your usage, as you cannot control event sequencing with a constraint.

If your labor calculation is assigned to the routing directly, it won't work at all. You will have to move the calculation into the profile, and simply use the result on the operation.

☞ QUESTION **95**

MC94 and Excel

How can I upload information from Excel to Flexible Planning (MC94)?

✍ ANSWER

It is possible but you have to be careful and exact in executing the procedure.

The essential thing to remember is that every aspect of the Excel file has to be exactly the same sequence and format as in MC94. This is not a formal SAP function; this is just a shortcut to copying large amounts of data in quick steps.

First step: from MC94, click Adjusted Quantity, then Key Figure. This expands the forecasts by line item. Control-F8 to change to your planning units (we always use meters). Then Edit-Sort Members-Ascending. Keep the MC94 screen in exactly this format for uploading later.

Download your plan into Excel by using Extras-Microsoft Excel. This will make a spreadsheet called Pt.xls. Save this under a new file name. You can update your forecast numbers in Excel in Pt.xls, but then you need to get them back up into SAP (this is pretty quick once you get some practice):

1. Reformat the Excel spreadsheet.

Highlight the data area in the spreadsheet. Use Data-Sort-Ascending by column A to get rid of the empty rows.

Hide all the columns for past months, i.e.: the first month showing should be next month, note: you can't upload previous month's forecasts.

Update your forecast numbers in this spreadsheet, manually or by copying in from other data from your sales staff.

2. Upload the Excel data to SAP MC94.

Have MC94 in exactly the same position as before, when you copied to Pt.xls.

For the entire visible table in MC94, i.e.: 17 rows (products), 10 columns (months), copy those rows and columns of data from your Excel spreadsheet, and paste into the top left cell of MC94. This will over-write all the visible data in MC94.

Then scroll down to the next set of 17 rows in MC94, and paste the next group of Excel data. At the end, check and save your data.

3. Comments.

This sounds awkward, but treat the visible areas of the MC94 table the same as the Excel table and it is just like copying data from one spreadsheet to another.

I use this especially for bulk changes, e.g.: add 10% to all forecasts in Excel and copy back into MC94 takes only a few minutes.

Just be very careful that both MC94 and Excel table are in the same sort sequence and in the same units, and make sure you line up the right products with the new forecasts.

☞ QUESTION **96**

Coverage Profile

Brief: I am creating a requirement through PIR on a monthly basis and I have configured a dynamic safety stock coverage profile of 7 days. The material is supplied to this plant from a warehouse and has been linked by a special procurement key. I have a similar dynamic safety stock coverage profile at the warehouse for 15 days.

Problem: I am unable to understand the calculation done by the SAP for raising the Purchase order. How is this done?

✐ ANSWER

Coverage profile is the tool used by SAP for dynamic safety stock.

Purchase Order (Requisition?) - is raised in the same way as usual with MRP, i.e.: calculated based on stock, planned receipts, orders & forecasts.

Dynamic safety stock (coverage profile) works by averaging the next sequence of forecasts and adding the equivalent of seven day's safety stock to the MRP requirements. So, if you have forecast of 30 units per month, SAP will add 7 units safety stock to the MRP calculation.

Have a look at help.sap by following this link:
http://help.sap.com/saphelp_40b/helpdata/es/36/e92c7dd435 d1118b3f0060b03ca329/content.htm

☞ QUESTION 97

Made to order, strategy group

I tried to implement the MTO strategy:

I have a configurable material X (FERT type, MRP type: PD, strategy group: 25 "Make-to-order for configurable material"). Its BOM depends on the results of configuration in sales order.

I then created the sales order, run MRP and I saw that for all of its components, there were created planned orders with reference to the sales order. Customer Stock appeared not only for the top-level material X but for its components too.

How do I avoid this? Shouldn't the special stockable type for sales order exist only for the top-level material?

✍ ANSWER

You can check and verify with the MRP4 view, field Individual/coll. It will show you the specifics you are looking for.

☞ QUESTION 98

Production Order Settlement

Can we do the Production ORDER Settlement to do Production Order itself?

If so, how do I go about it?

✍ ANSWER

Rework order is the best example for your question, where the rework order should get settled to Parent order.

In case of Collective orders, the system settles to a higher level order.

☞ **QUESTION 99**

Planning Horizon

Can we have planning horizon in 600 days?

This is required for one of our client in a peculiar environment.

✍ **ANSWER**

Planning Horizon is allowed up to 999 days. Field PLAHZ in standard SAP is defined for a length of 3 digits.

☞ QUESTION **100**

stock increase for finished products after CO11N

I use t-code: CO11N to perform production order confirmation, but I found no 101 record for the finished products generated (that means no stock increase to the finished products after confirmation). There were only 261 records generated for its components.

What went wrong and how do I resolve this?

✍ ANSWER

Before you save your confirmation, please click on Goods Movement button and check if you have got 101 for your finished product. If yes and still stock does not increase, then you will have to check COGI and see if there was any problem with the goods movement.

Also check material master properly in accounting. Make sure that you have maintained the valuation class properly.

INDEX

Attention SAP Experts

Have you ever considered writing a book in your area of SAP? Equity Press is the leading provider of knowledge products in SAP applications consulting, development, and support. If you have a manuscript or an idea of a manuscript, we'd love to help you get it published!

Please send your manuscript or manuscript ideas to jim@sapcookbook.com – we'll help you turn your dream into a reality.

Or mail your inquiries to:

Equity Press Manuscripts
BOX 706
Riverside, California
92502

Tel (951)788-0810
Fax (951)788-0812

50% Off your next
SAPCOOKBOOK order

If you plan of placing an order for 10 or more books from www.sapcookbook.com you qualify for volume discounts. Please send an email to books@sapcookbook.com or phone 951-788-0810 to place your order.

You can also fax your orders to 951-788-0812 .

Interview books are great for cross-training

In the new global economy, the more you know the better. The sharpest consultants are doing everything they can to pick up more than one functional area of SAP. Each of the following Certification Review / Interview Question books provides an excellent starting point for your module learning and investigation. These books get you started like no other book can – by providing you the information that you really need to know, and fast.

SAPCOOKBOOK Interview Questions, Answers, and Explanations

ABAP	-	SAP ABAP Certification Review: SAP ABAP Interview Questions, Answers, and Explanations
SD	-	SAP SD Interview Questions, Answers, and Explanations
Security	-	SAP Security: SAP Security Essentials
HR	-	mySAP HR Interview Questions, Answers, and Explanations: SAP HR Certification Review
BW	-	SAP BW Ultimate Interview Questions, Answers, and Explanations: SAW BW Certification Review
	-	SAP SRM Interview Questions Answers and Explanations
Basis	-	SAP Basis Certification Questions: Basis Interview Questions, Answers, and Explanations
MM	-	SAP MM Certification and Interview Questions: SAP MM Interview Questions, Answers, and Explanations

SAP BW Ultimate Interview Questions, Answers, and Explanations

Key Topics Include:

- The most important BW settings to know
- BW tables and transaction code quick references
- Certification Examination Questions
- Extraction, Modeling and Configuration
- Transformations and Administration
- Performance Tuning, Tips & Tricks, and FAQ
- Everything a BW resource needs to know before an interview

mySAP HR Interview Questions, Answers, and Explanations

Key topics include:

- The most important HR settings to know
- mySAP HR Administration tables and transaction code quick references
- SAP HR Certification Examination Questions
- Org plan, Compensation, Year End, Wages, and Taxes
- User Management, Transport System, Patches, and Upgrades
- Benefits, Holidays, Payroll, and Infotypes
- Everything an HR resource needs to know before an interview

SAP SRM Interview Questions, Answers, and Explanations

Key Topics Include:

- The most important SRM Configuration to know
- Common EBP Implementation Scenarios
- Purchasing Document Approval Processes
- Supplier Self Registration and Self Service (SUS)
- Live Auctions and Bidding Engine, RFX Processes (LAC)
- Details for Business Intelligence and Spend Analysis
- EBP Technical and Troubleshooting Information

SAP MM Interview Questions, Answers, and Explanations

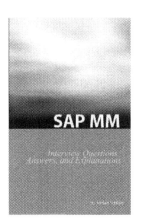

- The most important MM Configuration to know
- Common MM Implementation Scenarios
- MM Certification Exam Questions
- Consumption Based Planning
- Warehouse Management
- Material Master Creation and Planning
- Purchasing Document Inforecords

SAP SD Interview Questions, Answers, and Explanations

- The most important SD settings to know
- SAP SD administration tables and transaction code quick references
- SAP SD Certification Examination Questions
- Sales Organization and Document Flow Introduction
- Partner Procedures, Backorder Processing, Sales BOM
- Backorder Processing, Third Party Ordering, Rebates and Refunds
- Everything an SD resource needs to know before an interview

SAP Basis Interview Questions, Answers, and Explanations

- The most important Basis settings to know
- Basis Administration tables and transaction code quick references
- Certification Examination Questions
- Oracle database, UNIX, and MS Windows Technical Information
- User Management, Transport System, Patches, and Upgrades
- Backup and Restore, Archiving, Disaster Recover, and Security
- Everything a Basis resource needs to know before an interview

SAP Security Essentials

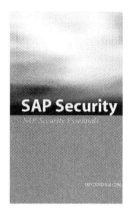

- Finding Audit Critical Combinations
- Authentication, Transaction Logging, and Passwords
- Roles, Profiles, and User Management
- ITAR, DCAA, DCMA, and Audit Requirements
- The most important security settings to know
- Security Tuning, Tips & Tricks, and FAQ
- Transaction code list and table name references

SAP Workflow Interview Questions, Answers, and Explanations

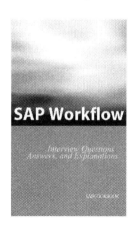

- Database Updates and Changing the Standard
- List Processing, Internal Tables, and ALV Grid Control
- Dialog Programming, ABAP Objects
- Data Transfer, Basis Administration
- ABAP Development reference updated for 2006!
- Everything an ABAP resource needs to know before an interview

www.ingramcontent.com/pod-product-compliance
Lightning Source LLC
Chambersburg PA
CBHW051246050326
40689CB00007B/1092